Disney

LEARN TO DRAW

GOOFY and Pluto

Illustrated by
Todd Kurosawa
Pattie Tomsicek
Diana Wakeman

Hi, Friends!

Let's get ready to draw those two comical characters, Goofy and Pluto. You'll be amazed at how quickly and easily you'll learn the techniques used by the professionals. And you'll have a great time doing it! First, you'll need a few basic supplies. Let's go over them with the gang!

OF COURSE YOU'LL NEED PENCILS TO DRAW. TRY TO PICK UP SOME NUMBER 2 PENCILS. THEY WILL BE THE MOST USEFUL.

HAVE AN ERASER ON HAND. YOU'LL NEED IT TO REMOVE ANY MISTAKES AND TO CLEAN UP YOUR SKETCHES AS YOU GO ALONG.

BE SURE THAT YOU HAVE A PENCIL SHARPENER. DULL PENCILS MAKE DULL DRAWINGS!

YOU'RE GOING TO GO THROUGH A FAIR AMOUNT OF PAPER. SO WHY NOT GET YOURSELF A SKETCH PAD?

FELT-TIP PENS COME IN A NUMBER OF SHAPES, SIZES, AND COLORS. PICK UP A VARIETY. YOU'LL NEED BLACK FELT-TIPS TO OUTLINE YOUR DRAWING AND COLORED ONES TO ADD THE COLOR AFTERWARDS.

Getting the Right Shapes

If you can draw a few very simple shapes, you can draw Goofy and Pluto! Keep drawing your lines and shapes, over and over, on top of each other, until the right shape appears.

DRAW LINES WITH DIFFERENT CURVES — SMOOTH CURVES AND SHARP ONES. DRAW LOTS OF THEM TOGETHER.

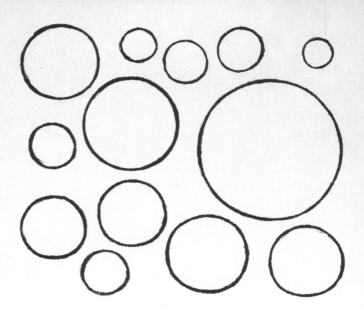

LIGHTLY DRAW AROUND AND AROUND UNTIL NICE, ROUND CIRCLES START TO FORM. DRAW CIRCLES IN DIFFERENT SIZES.

AN OVAL LOOKS LIKE A CIRCLE THAT HAS BEEN STRETCHED OR SQUASHED. DRAW DIFFERENT-SIZED OVALS.

DRAW CIRCLES AND CURVED LINES THAT CONNECT TO MAKE PEAR SHAPES.

Finishing Off

Daisy, Donald and Minnie are busy drawing Goofy! Let's see how it's done.

FIRST DAISY SKETCHES GOOFY WITH HER #2 PENCIL. KEEP THOSE LINES LIGHT AND SMOOTH, DAISY!

IT LOOKS AS THOUGH DONALD IS GETTING A LITTLE CARRIED AWAY AS HE REMOVES UNWANTED PENCIL LINES WITH HIS ERASER AND CLEANS UP THE SKETCH. TRY A SOFTER TOUCH, DONALD!

MINNIE'S FINISHING UP BY OUTLINING THE DRAWING IN BLACK, LETTING THE LINES DRY, AND THEN ADDING THE COLOR. NICE JOB, MINNIE!

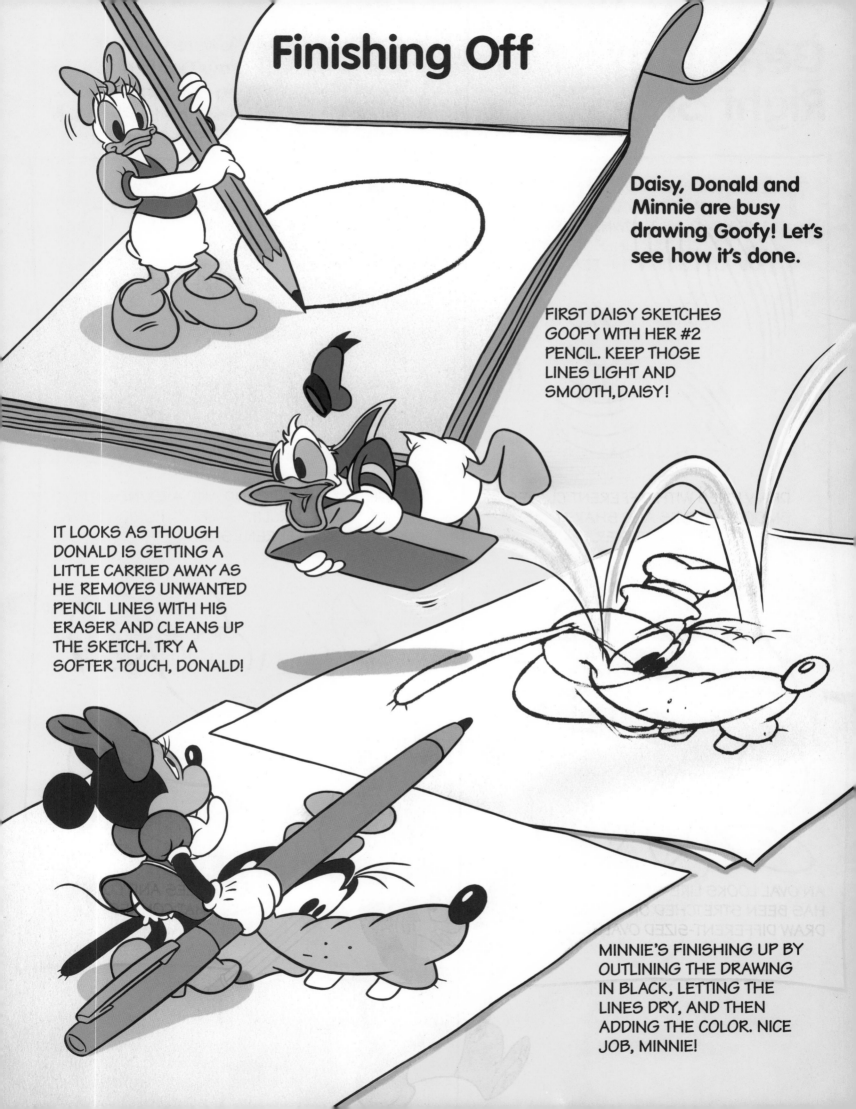

Let's Draw Goofy's Face

Goofy's face has a lot of character. But you'll be able to capture him perfectly by using the simple shapes you've already learned. Each new step you'll need to make is shown in blue.

1 LIGHTLY DRAW A CIRCLE FOR GOOFY'S HEAD. WRAP TWO CURVED LINES AROUND THE HEAD AS SHOWN. THESE ARE CALLED "CENTER LINES." THEY'LL HELP YOU TO POSITION THE FEATURES.

2 FOR GOOFY'S EYES, DRAW TWO OVALS, ONE ON EITHER SIDE OF THE CENTER LINE. FOR HIS MUZZLE, DRAW A LARGE CONE SHAPE BELOW THE EYES, USING STRAIGHT AND CURVED LINES. ADD A CURVED BUMP TO THE TOP OF HIS HEAD.

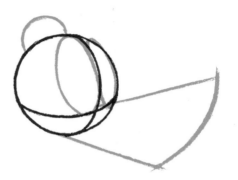

5 USE CURVES TO DRAW GOOFY'S CHEEK, CHIN, LIP, AND THE CORNER OF HIS MOUTH. DRAW OVALS TO ADD HIS NOSE AND ITS HIGHLIGHT. FINISH DRAWING HIS HAT USING CURVED LINES.

6 ADD GOOFY'S HAIR, EARS, TEETH AND WHISKERS, USING CURVES AND DOTS. REMEMBER TO KEEP GOOFY'S PERSONALITY IN MIND WHILE YOU DRAW.

Remember, draw lightly and smoothly until you get the right shapes.

3 DRAW TWO OVALS FOR GOOFY'S PUPILS. FORM HIS BROWS WITH TWO CURVED LINES ABOVE THE EYES. MAKE GOOFY'S CHIN WITH A CURVED LINE RUNNING FROM THE CIRCLE TO THE MUZZLE SHAPE.

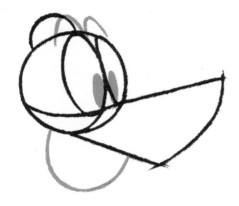

4 GOOFY'S HAT FITS SNUGLY OVER THE BUMP ON HIS HEAD! USING CURVES, COVER THE BUMP WITH A CUP SHAPE. FIT A TUBE INTO THE CUP, AND TOP IT OFF WITH AN OVAL.

NOW, GIVE GOOFY'S MUZZLE ITS ROUNDED, BUMPY SHAPE BY DRAWING A SERIES OF CURVES.

7 GENTLY ERASE THE CONSTRUCTION LINES AND ANY OTHER STRAY PENCIL MARKS UNTIL YOU'RE LEFT WITH A NEAT, CLEAN DRAWING.

8 OUTLINE AND FILL IN THE DARK AREAS WITH BLACK. LET THE INK DRY, AND THEN COLOR IN GOOFY!

Let's Draw Pluto

Pluto is a wonderful character to draw. His enthusiasm is contagious! To draw Pluto, you use the same curves, circles, ovals and pear shapes you've been practicing.

1 START WITH A LIGHT CIRCLE FOR PLUTO'S HEAD. ADD TWO CURVED CENTER LINES THAT WRAP AROUND THE CIRCLE.

2 USE TWO CURVED LINES TO DRAW PLUTO'S NECK. USE MORE CURVES TO DRAW PLUTO'S COLLAR. PLUTO'S COLLAR HANGS LOOSELY AROUND HIS NECK, LIKE A BIG RING.

5 GIVE PLUTO'S MUZZLE ITS ROUNDED, BUMPY SHAPE BY ADDING A SERIES OF CURVES.

6 USE CURVED LINES TO FORM THE CHEEK, THE CORNER OF THE MOUTH, THE LIP, CHIN, AND THE FOLD WHERE THE EAR CONNECTS TO THE HEAD. ADD THE THIN, DROOPY EARS, AND DOTS FOR THE WHISKERS.

Follow the simple steps below. The colored lines show each new step you need to make. Be sure to keep your pencil sharp and draw lightly!

3 DRAW OVALS ON EITHER SIDE OF THE CENTER LINE TO MAKE PLUTO'S EYES. MAKE HIS MUZZLE BY DRAWING A CONE SHAPE BELOW THE EYES. ADD A CURVED BUMP TO THE TOP OF PLUTO'S HEAD.

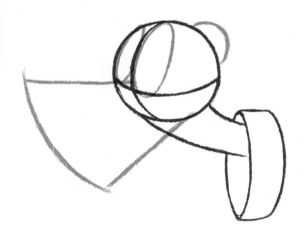

4 DRAW OVALS FOR PLUTO'S PUPILS. FORM THE BROWS WITH TWO CURVED LINES ABOVE THE EYES. CREATE AN EDGE ON THE COLLAR BY ADDING ONE MORE CURVED LINE ON THE INSIDE OF THE RING.

7 CAREFULLY ERASE ANY UNWANTED LINES AND CLEAN UP THE DRAWING.

8 OUTLINE AND FILL IN THE DARK AREAS WITH BLACK. AFTER THE INK DRIES, USE YOUR FELT-TIP PENS TO COLOR IN PLUTO!

Goofy's Expressions

Goofy's face is soft and flexible. He can squash and stretch his features to express dozens of attitudes and expressions.

WOW! DOESN'T GOOFY LOOK *SURPRISED* WHEN YOU DRAW HIM WITH HIS WHOLE HEAD STRETCHED UP, HIS EYES WIDE OPEN, AND HIS EARS RISING IN THE AIR?

TO MAKE AN *ANGRY GOOFY*, BRING THE CENTER OF HIS BROW *DOWN* OVER THE EYES, LOWER THE CHEEKS, AND ADD A FROWN.

GOOFY WILL LOOK *SLEEPY* IF YOU LOWER HIS EYELIDS AND MOUTH, AND CROSS HIS PUPILS. HIS EARS SHOULD DROOP TO COMPLETE THE TIRED LOOK.

DRAW A *HAPPY GOOFY* BY OPENING HIS MOUTH, LIFTING HIS CHEEKS AND GIVING HIS EYES A MERRY SQUINT. ADD SWINGING EARS FOR A JOLLY TOUCH!

Let's Draw Hands

Goofy always wears white gloves. His hand is basically a circle with long, sausage-like fingers and a shorter, rounder thumb.

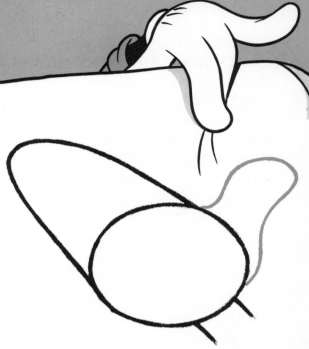

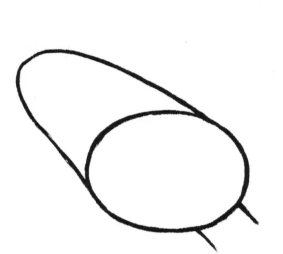

1 LIGHTLY DRAW A CIRCLE FOR THE PALM OF THE HAND. ADD A CURVED LINE GOING FROM ONE SIDE OF THE CIRCLE TO THE OTHER. THIS FORMS THE BASIC SHAPE OF THE FINGERS. ADD TWO LINES FOR THE ARM.

2 CURVE THE BASE OF THE THUMB AROUND TOWARDS THE ARM AND THEN BRING IT IN TO JOIN THE CIRCLE.

3 FORM THE FINGERS BY DRAWING STRETCHED OVALS, LIKE SAUSAGES. ADD A CUFF TO THE GLOVE.

4 DRAW IN THE PALM LINE. GENTLY ERASE THE CONSTRUCTION LINES AND CLEAN UP THE DRAWING.

Goofy Standing

Goofy is seven and a half head-circles tall. This means that if you stack seven and a half Goofy heads on top of each other, that is how tall Goofy should be.

1 LIGHTLY DRAW THE LINE OF ACTION. DRAW A CIRCLE FOR THE HEAD AND A LONG PEAR SHAPE FOR THE BODY. ADD CURVED CENTER LINES TO THE HEAD AND CONNECT THE HEAD TO THE BODY WITH A CURVED NECK. NOTICE THAT GOOFY HAS A CURVED SPINE AND THAT HIS HEAD AND NECK LEAN FORWARD.

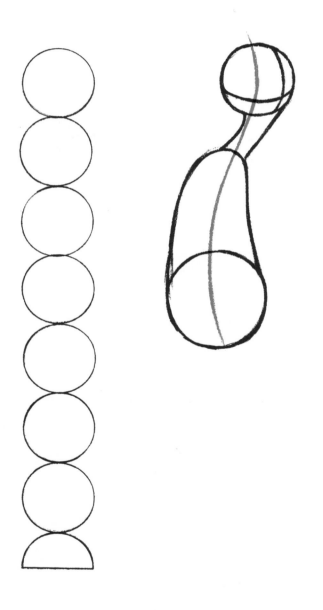

2 DRAW TUBE SHAPES FOR THE ARMS AND LEGS, BENDING THEM AT THE ELBOWS AND KNEES. USE OVALS TO DRAW THE HANDS. ADD THE FEET BY DRAWING OVALS FOR THE HEELS AND TOES AND CONNECTING THEM WITH CURVED LINES.

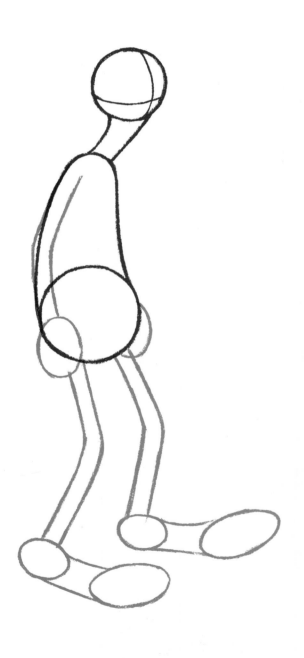

Whenever you are drawing the whole figure, you should start with the line of action. This is a guideline that will help you give your character direction and movement.

3 ADD THE FACIAL FEATURES AND THE HAT AS YOU LEARNED BEFORE.

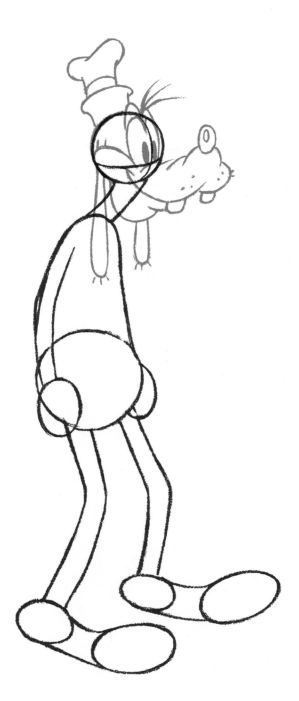

4 USE CURVED LINES AND OVALS TO DRAW THE BASIC SHAPES OF GOOFY'S CLOTHES. NOTICE THAT THE SLEEVES AND PANT LEGS ARE LIKE TUBES, AND THAT THE COLLAR AND CUFFS ARE LIKE RINGS.

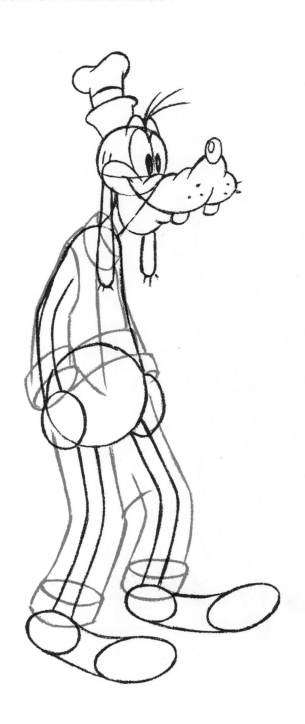

Goofy Standing

Goofy's clothes are an important part of his character. You can see why you should draw Goofy's clothes with just as much care and feeling as you would draw his face and hands.

5 ADD THE DETAILS TO GOOFY'S CLOTHING. THE CURVED LINES THAT CREATE FOLDS GIVE GOOFY A SOFT, ROUNDED FEELING AND ADD PERSONALITY.

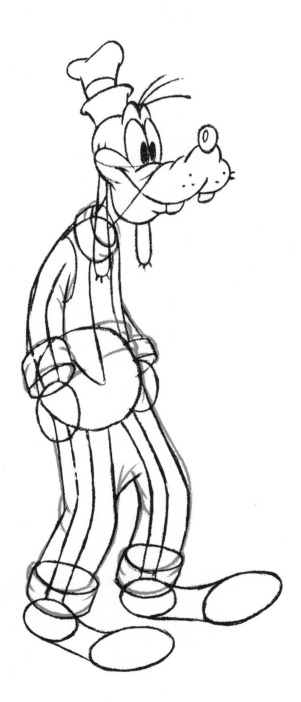

6 DRAW IN THE DETAILS OF GOOFY'S SHOES AND GLOVES. USE A SERIES OF CURVES TO GIVE GOOFY'S SHOES THEIR ROUND, LUMPY LOOK. ADD THE TINY HEELS AND THE THIN, WORN SOLES.

7 USE YOUR ERASER TO GENTLY REMOVE ANY UNWANTED LINES AND CLEAN UP THE DRAWING.

8 OUTLINE THE DRAWING AND FILL IN THE DARK AREAS WITH BLACK. LET THE INK DRY, ADD COLOR WITH YOUR FELT-TIP PENS, AND YOU'RE DONE!

Pluto Standing

One way that Pluto differs from Goofy is that he stands on all four legs. Pluto is three and a half heads high to the top of his shoulder. This means that if you stack three and a half circles of equal size on top of each other, that is how high his shoulder should be. His body is four heads long from his shoulder to his rear.

1

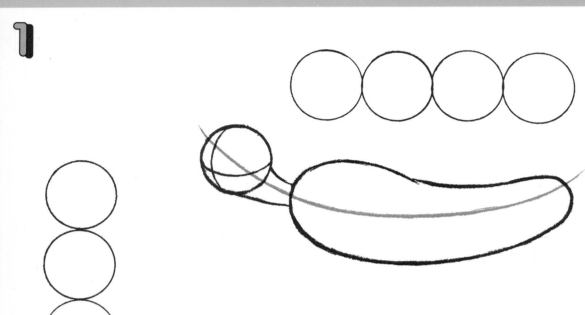

LIGHTLY DRAW THE LINE OF ACTION. DRAW A CIRCLE FOR PLUTO'S HEAD AND A LONG, STRETCHED-OUT PEAR SHAPE FOR HIS BODY. CONNECT THE TWO SHAPES BY DRAWING THE NECK. NOTICE THAT PLUTO'S NECK IS WIDER AT THE HEAD THAN AT THE BODY.

3

DRAW IN THE ROUNDED SHAPE OF PLUTO'S TOES AND ADD CURVED LINES TO FORM HIS ELBOW AND THE CREASES AT THE TOPS OF HIS LEGS. ADD A CURVED TAIL. DRAW IN THE FACE AS YOU LEARNED BEFORE.

Whenever you want to draw a complete figure, you should start by drawing the line of action. The line of action is a guideline that will help you to give your character direction and movement.

2

DRAW CURVED SHOULDERS AND TUBE-LIKE LEGS. ADD OVALS FOR THE BASIC SHAPE OF THE PAWS.

4

USE YOUR ERASER TO GENTLY REMOVE THE CONSTRUCTION LINES AND STRAY PENCIL MARKS. OUTLINE YOUR DRAWING AND FILL IN THE DARK AREAS WITH BLACK. LET THE INK DRY, AND YOU'RE READY TO COLOR!

More Hands

You'll want to be able to draw hands in every possible position. After practicing these hands, make up some of your own!

NOTICE THE THREE LINES ON THE BACK OF GOOFY'S HAND. THESE LINES FOLLOW THE ROUNDED SHAPE OF THE GLOVE.

Pluto's Expressions

By stretching and squashing Pluto's eyes, mouth, and ears, you can convey the full range of his emotions.

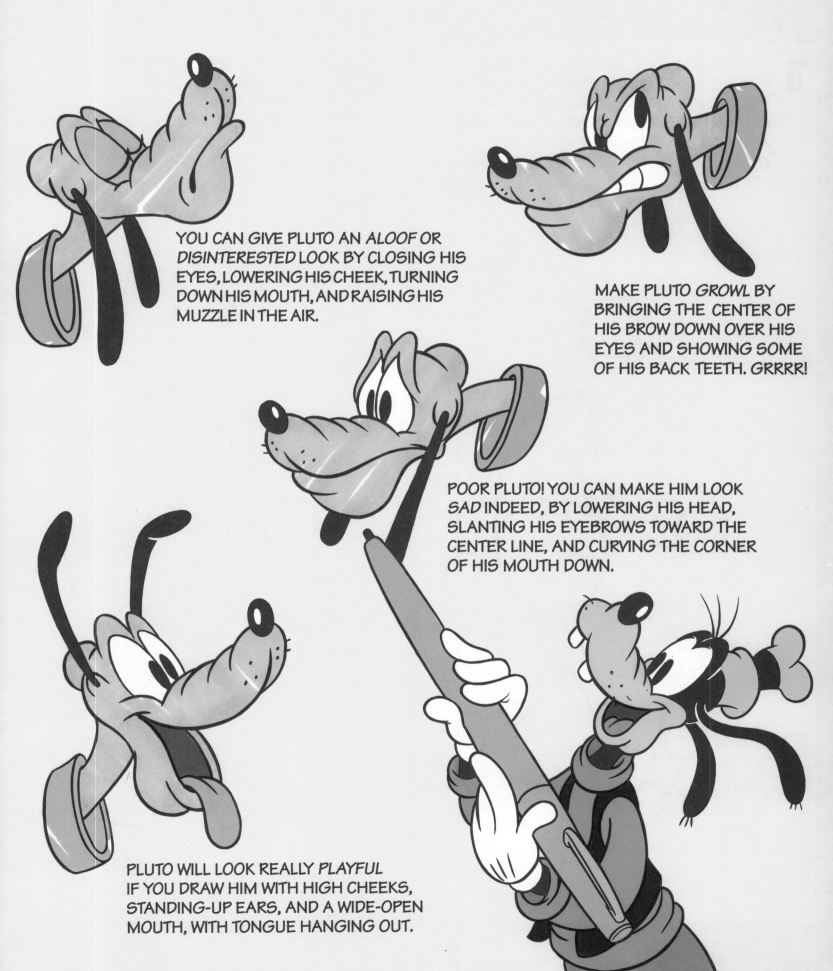

YOU CAN GIVE PLUTO AN *ALOOF* OR *DISINTERESTED* LOOK BY CLOSING HIS EYES, LOWERING HIS CHEEK, TURNING DOWN HIS MOUTH, AND RAISING HIS MUZZLE IN THE AIR.

MAKE PLUTO *GROWL* BY BRINGING THE CENTER OF HIS BROW DOWN OVER HIS EYES AND SHOWING SOME OF HIS BACK TEETH. GRRRR!

POOR PLUTO! YOU CAN MAKE HIM LOOK SAD INDEED, BY LOWERING HIS HEAD, SLANTING HIS EYEBROWS TOWARD THE CENTER LINE, AND CURVING THE CORNER OF HIS MOUTH DOWN.

PLUTO WILL LOOK REALLY *PLAYFUL* IF YOU DRAW HIM WITH HIGH CHEEKS, STANDING-UP EARS, AND A WIDE-OPEN MOUTH, WITH TONGUE HANGING OUT.

Goofy Walking

The line of action is crucial in action poses. If your drawings don't start with a sense of life, they'll never have it, however nicely you add the details. So be sure

1 DRAW THE LINE OF ACTION. ADD A CIRCLE FOR THE HEAD AND A LONG PEAR SHAPE FOR THE BODY. NEXT, DRAW IN THE CURVED CENTER LINES. ADD THE ARMS AND LEGS. ADD OVALS FOR THE HANDS AND SETS OF OVALS, CONNECTED BY CURVES, FOR THE FEET.

2 DRAW IN THE CONE FOR THE BASIC SHAPE OF THE MUZZLE. ADD A CURVED LINE FOR THE CHIN. DRAW OVALS FOR THE EYES, AS YOU LEARNED TO DO EARLIER. ADD THE CLOTHES.

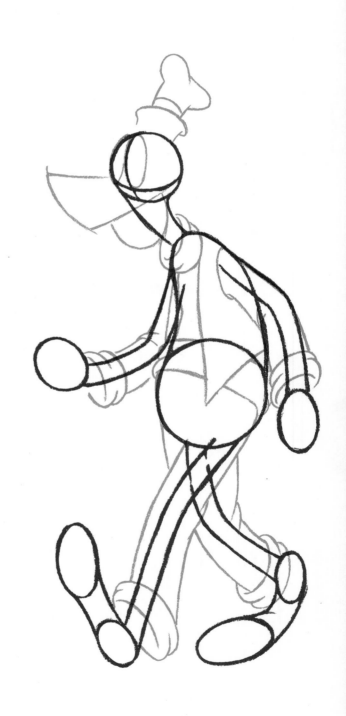

to give the initial steps as much feeling as you can. And remember, draw lightly!

3 DRAW IN THE DETAILS FOR THE HEAD. ADD THE DETAILS ON THE GLOVES AND THE SHOES. NOTICE HOW FLEXIBLE GOOFY'S HANDS AND FEET ARE AS THEY MOVE.

4 GENTLY ERASE THE CONSTRUCTION LINES AND ANY OTHER STRAY PENCIL MARKS. OUTLINE YOUR DRAWING AND FILL IN THE DARK AREAS WITH BLACK. LET THE INK DRY, AND THEN COLOR IN GOOFY!

Pluto Running

Pluto is a non-stop kind of dog. Your drawing should look as if you've caught him in mid-action. Give Pluto the energy he needs with a big, curved line of action.

1

LIGHTLY DRAW THE LINE OF ACTION. ADD A CIRCLE FOR THE HEAD AND A LONG, STRETCHED PEAR SHAPE FOR THE BODY. DRAW IN CURVED CENTER LINES. NEXT, ADD THE NECK, LEGS, AND PAWS.

3

ADD THE DETAILS OF THE FACE, BODY, AND PAWS. FORM THE UNDERSIDE OF PLUTO'S PAWS WITH THREE SMALL OVALS AND A CURVED LINE. BE SURE TO GIVE SOME LIFE TO PLUTO'S TAIL.

2

DRAW OVALS FOR PLUTO'S EYES AND CURVED LINES FOR THE COLLAR. ADD THE BUMP ON TOP OF HIS HEAD. DRAW IN THE BASIC CONE SHAPE OF THE MUZZLE.

4

CAREFULLY REMOVE THE UNWANTED LINES WITH YOUR ERASER AND CLEAN UP THE DRAWING. OUTLINE AND FILL IN THE DARK AREAS IN BLACK. AFTER THE INK DRIES, GIVE COLOR TO PLUTO WITH YOUR FELT-TIP PENS!

Action Poses

A sense of action gives your drawings life and makes them fun to look at. Try drawing Goofy and Pluto in the poses below, and then make up some of your own.

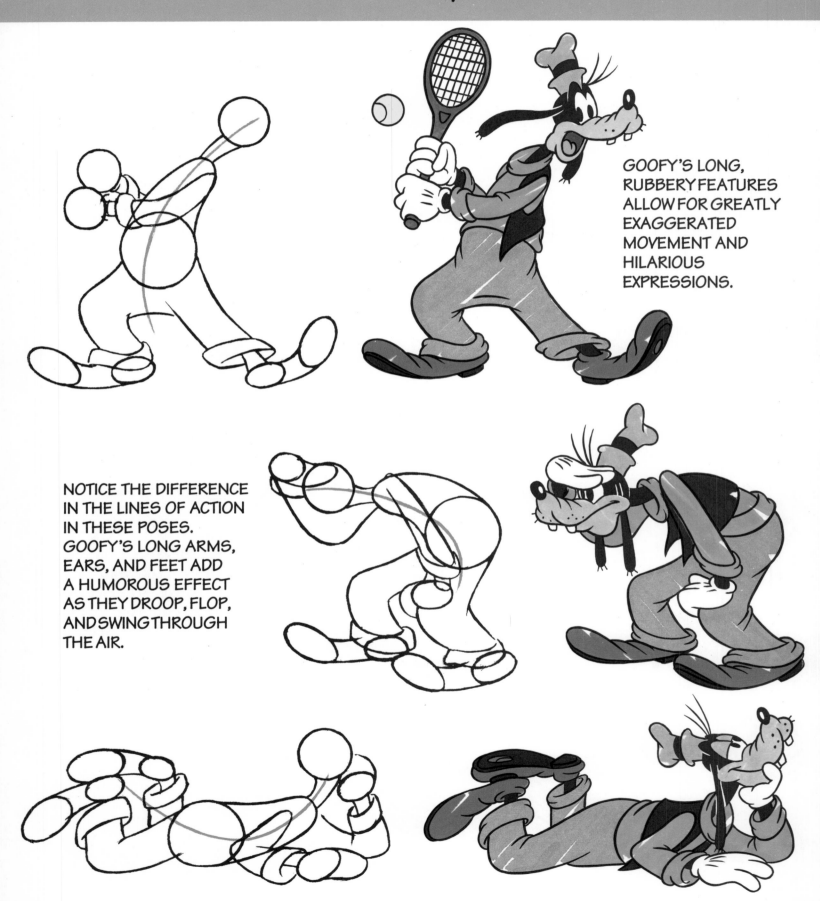

GOOFY'S LONG, RUBBERY FEATURES ALLOW FOR GREATLY EXAGGERATED MOVEMENT AND HILARIOUS EXPRESSIONS.

NOTICE THE DIFFERENCE IN THE LINES OF ACTION IN THESE POSES. GOOFY'S LONG ARMS, EARS, AND FEET ADD A HUMOROUS EFFECT AS THEY DROOP, FLOP, AND SWING THROUGH THE AIR.

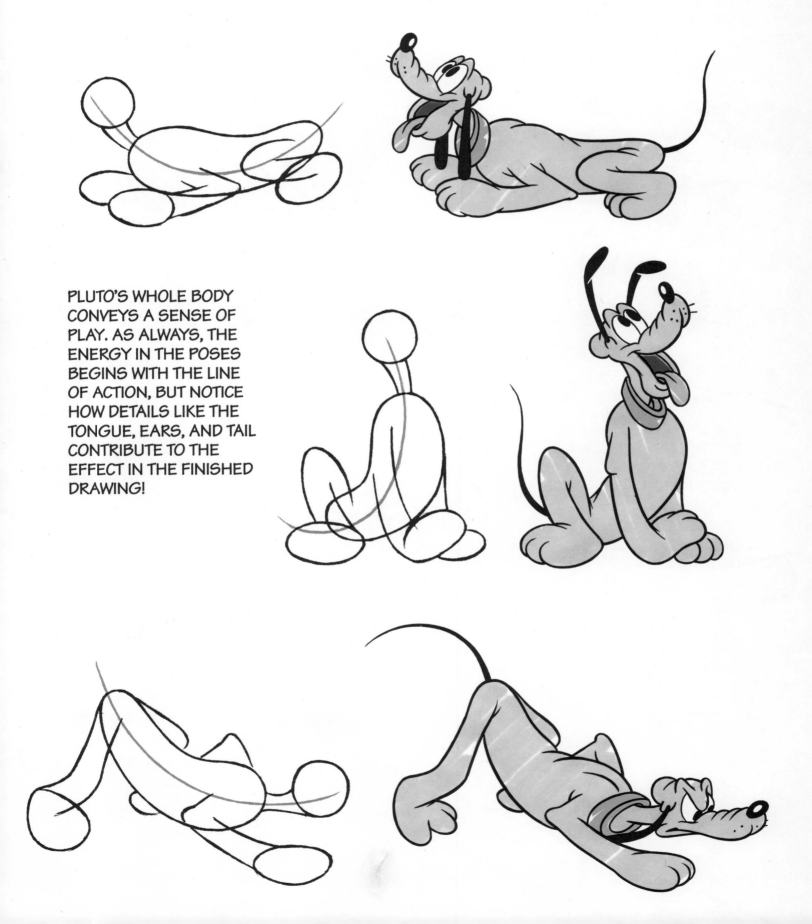

PLUTO'S WHOLE BODY CONVEYS A SENSE OF PLAY. AS ALWAYS, THE ENERGY IN THE POSES BEGINS WITH THE LINE OF ACTION, BUT NOTICE HOW DETAILS LIKE THE TONGUE, EARS, AND TAIL CONTRIBUTE TO THE EFFECT IN THE FINISHED DRAWING!

Coloring Tips

Mickey and Chip and Dale are coming up with some beautiful results as they color in pictures of Pluto and Goofy.

MICKEY IS USING THE VERY TIP OF HIS BLACK FELT-TIP MARKER TO GIVE PLUTO A CRISP, CLEAN OUTLINE. WHEN HE ADDS THE COLOR HE TILTS HIS MARKER AT AN ANGLE SO THAT THE BROADER SIDE OF THE TIP GIVES HIM BETTER COVERAGE.

CHIP AND DALE HAVE THE RIGHT IDEA! THEY'VE GOT GOOFY'S FEET PLANTED FIRMLY ON THE GROUND. THE WISPS OF GRASS AND THE BRICK WALL ARE ALL THAT IS NEEDED TO SUGGEST A WHOLE WORLD SURROUNDING GOOFY.

Other Ways to Color

There are lots of different materials you can use to color Goofy and Pluto. Here are just some examples.

NOTHING SEEMS TO COME EASILY FOR POOR DONALD! BUT THAT'S WHY WE LOVE HIM. YOU'RE SURE TO HAVE NO TROUBLE AT ALL FINISHING OFF YOUR PICTURES WITH A BRUSH AND A TRAY OF WATERCOLORS!

MICKEY'S A REAL WHIZ WHEN HE GETS HIS HANDS ON A COUPLE OF COLORED PENCILS. WHY DON'T YOU GIVE THEM A TRY?

IT LOOKS AS THOUGH GOOFY'S GETTING HIS FEET WET WITH SOME POSTER PAINTS. YOU MIGHT WANT TO TRY A SLIGHTLY MORE CONTROLLED TECHNIQUE TO FINISH OFF YOUR DRAWINGS. YOU'LL FIND THAT POSTER PAINTS ARE LOTS OF FUN!

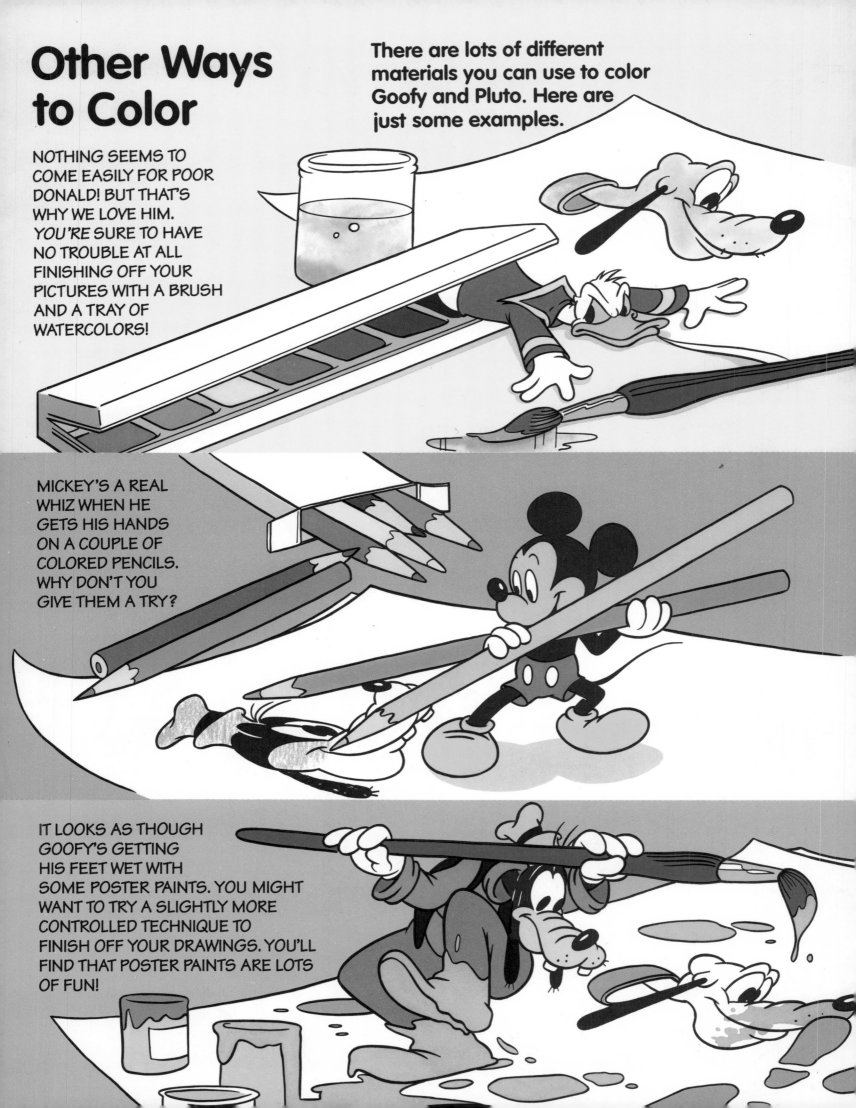